21st Century Junior Library

WORKING AT THE ZOO

by Tamra Orr

CHERRY LAKE PUBLISHING * ANN ARBOR, MICHIGAN

Published in the United States of America by Cherry Lake Publishing
Ann Arbor, Michigan
www.cherrylakepublishing.com

Content Adviser: Steve Feldman, Association of Zoos and Aquariums
Reading Adviser: Cecilia Minden-Cupp, PhD, Literacy Consultant

Photo Credits: Cover, ©Scott Leman/Shutterstock, Inc. and ©Bork/Shutterstock, Inc.; cover and
page 6, ©iStockphoto.com/WoodenDinosaur; cover and page 12, ©iStockphoto.com/49pauly;
page 4, ©Bluerain/Shutterstock, Inc.; page 8, ©Will Parson/Shutterstock, Inc.; page 10, ©Kondrachov
Vladimir/Shutterstock, Inc.; page 14, ©PCL/Alamy; page 16, ©Elena Stepanova/Shutterstock, Inc.;
page 18, ©iStockphoto.com/hartcreations; page 20, ©Josef Muellek/Dreamstime.com

LIBRARY OF CONGRESS CATALOGING-IN-PUBLICATION DATA
Orr, Tamra.
 Working at the zoo/by Tamra Orr.
  p. cm.—(21st century junior library)
 Includes bibliographical references and index.
 ISBN-13: 978-1-60279-978-3 (lib. bdg.)
 ISBN-10: 1-60279-978-4 (lib. bdg.)
 1. Zoo keepers—Juvenile literature. 2. Zoos—Juvenile literature.
 3. Zoo animals—Juvenile literature. I. Title. II. Series.
 QL50.5.O77 2011
 590.7'3—dc22   2010030571

Cherry Lake Publishing would like to acknowledge the work of
The Partnership for 21st Century Skills.
Please visit www.21stcenturyskills.org for more information.

Printed in the United States of America
Corporate Graphics Inc.
January 2011
CLSP08

CONTENTS

Workers make sure the chimps have plenty of things to climb on.

What Is a Zoo?

Look over there! It's a tiger. Look at its black stripes. Do you see that snake? It is sunning itself on the rock. Maybe it is watching the **chimpanzees** swing around their **enclosure**. Welcome to the zoo!

Some zoo workers help keep animals clean.

There are zoos all over the world.
Zoos give people a chance to see animals
up close.

Many people work at zoos. They help
visitors learn and have fun. They also
work hard to keep the animals healthy
and safe.

You might get a close-up view of your favorite
animal at the zoo!

Zoo Workers

You will see many animals at the zoo. You will not see all the workers. Many of them work in areas that are not open to zoo visitors.

Ask Questions! Which animals need the most care? Which ones are the most fun to watch? Do you have questions about the zoo? Ask the workers. You may learn something new about zoos!

Zoo directors need to know how to care for all kinds of animals.

The zoo **director** is in charge of the zoo. This job can be hard. A zoo director has to know about all of the animals in the zoo.

Each animal needs its own special care. The director needs to make sure everyone who works at the zoo does a good job.

Veterinarians need to know how to give medicine to animals.

Zookeepers take care of the animals. They give the animals fresh food and water. They also make sure the animals' cages and enclosures are clean.

Zookeepers are the first to notice when an animal isn't feeling well. Then they ask the zoo's **veterinarian** for help.

Think!

Would you like to take care of animals? What would you need to know about animals? What classes would you take in high school or college? Most zookeepers study sciences called **biology** and **zoology**.

Zoos around the world have maintenance crews to keep them looking good.

The zoo's **maintenance crew** makes sure the zoo looks tidy and clean. They fix anything that has broken. **Gardeners** trim bushes and trees. They also pull weeds and water plants. The maintenance crew and gardeners work together to keep the zoo clean and safe for visitors.

Look!

Look around the next time you are at the zoo. Do you see a lot of plants? Plants help keep the animals happy and comfortable. What kind of care do you think plants need?

Snack bar workers can sell you treats such as cotton candy.

Not everyone at the zoo works with animals. Some of the workers help people who come to see the animals.

You often need a ticket to enter the zoo. Workers take your money at the ticket window. Other people work in the gift shop. There are also workers at the snack bar.

Taking care of a pet is a fun way to learn more about an animal.

Do You Want to Work at a Zoo?

Does working at a zoo sound like fun? You can start getting ready now.

Do you have a pet? Taking care of a pet is a great way to get started. If you don't have a pet, maybe you can help take care of a neighbor's pet.

Do you want to work at a zoo?

Learn as much as you can about all kinds of animals. Your local zoo might have programs you can attend. Library books and Web sites have information about animal care. You can also learn from nature shows on television.

Maybe one day you will work at the zoo!

GLOSSARY

biology (bye-OL-uh-jee) the study of living things

chimpanzees (chim-pan-ZEEZ) small apes that come from Africa

director (duh-REK-tur) the head of an organization such as a zoo

enclosure (en-KLOH-zhur) a closed-off area where animals live

gardeners (GARD-uhn-urz) people who take care of plants

maintenance crew (MAYN-tuh-nuhnss KROO) a group of workers who take care of a zoo's buildings, outdoor areas, and equipment

veterinarian (vet-ur-uh-NAIR-ee-uhn) a doctor trained to treat animals

zookeepers (ZOO-kee-purz) people in charge of a zoo's animals

zoology (zoo-AH-luh-jee) the scientific study of animals

FIND OUT MORE

BOOKS

Harrison, Sarah. *A Day at a Zoo*. Minneapolis: Millbrook Press, 2009.

Markarian, Margie. *Who Scoops Elephant Poo? Working at a Zoo*. Chicago: Raintree, 2011.

Sweeney, Alyse. *Who Works at the Zoo?* New York: Children's Press, 2007.

WEB SITES

Association of Zoos and Aquariums
www.aza.org
Find a local zoo, read about different kinds of animals, and check out the latest news about zoos.

American Association of Zoo Keepers
www.aazk.org
Learn more about zookeepers and their jobs.

INDEX

ABOUT THE AUTHOR

Tamra Orr is the author of more than 250 books for children. She and her family live in Portland, Oregon, where there is a fabulous zoo! With a dog, a cat, and three teenagers, she is sure that she knows just what it takes to run a zoo.